the Little Book of
Awareness

Being aware of being aware
is the essence of enlightenment

Peter Ingle

The Little Book of Awareness

Awareness

Copyright © 2011–2019 by Peter Ingle
All Rights Reserved

No part of this publication may be reproduced, store, or transmitted, in any form, or by any means, electronic, mechanical, photocopying, recording, or otherwise, without permission in writing from the author.

Library of Congress Cataloging-in-Publication Data

Ingle, Peter M.
Awareness

ISBN 978-0-9746349-3-7
Produced in the United States

Foreword

The mind is a jar that contains things. Those things are what we know and experience as thoughts, sensations, and emotions. They include ideas, opinions, decisions, reactions, doubts, fears, expectations, anxieties, pain, and hurt—the full gamut of our psychological *interpretation* of living. It is all there in the jar where lighter things rise to the top and heavier ones sink to the thick bottom.

The jar of the mind also houses an invisible medium in which everything is suspended, like fish in the sea. This medium is best described as a simple degree of awareness that vivifies whatever it comes into contact with.

Neither the jar nor its contents are aware of themselves. They are always known *through* the medium of awareness. The only thing that can be aware of itself is the medium, but even it is usually unaware of what it really is.

When the contents of the jar are rendered more quiet and still, the awareness surrounding them naturally withdraws its consciousness *of things* back into itself. In doing so it becomes aware of being aware and realizes itself as the 'light' that makes everything else visible.

Significantly, however, awareness is not visible even to itself. It simply becomes aware of being aware, but never as a thought, an inner voice, an impulse, a sensation, or an emotion of *any* kind. Rather, it emerges as a formless, motionless, silent presence with the capacity to be consciously aware. It just sees and is aware of seeing. What this fully implies is indescribable because it is so completely other than the mind and all the contents of the mind (and body).

This awareness in our mind is like the air inside a room, which is independent of the furniture and of the room itself in the same way that the air outside is independent of all the objects in the world. There is also no lid on the jar of our mind preventing awareness from escaping into the sky of its larger Self. The only thing that keeps awareness mind-ridden is its own fascination with the things around it. The more it remains fascinated with—and hence fastened to—the contents of the jar, the more those contents appropriate awareness for themselves in myriad forms of 'I', 'me', and 'mine'—the ego self.

This false appropriation is the number one dilemma for awareness. But it does not have to force its way out of the jar. It has simply to realize itself as awareness, let go its hold of things, start rising, and keep expanding as its endless Self of the universe.

TO BE AWARE of being aware is the essence of enlightenment.

True masters are masters of awareness. They are not interested in getting hold of the world. They want to get hold of their real selves, their conscious awareness. Nothing is more interesting or worthwhile.

Awareness is not ordinarily aware of itself. It is always there. It is simply unaware of being there.

When awareness becomes aware of being aware, it realizes that it is always there. It self-realizes.

The mind looks for meaning in things without recognizing that awareness is what gives meaning to everything. This is why the mind is never satisfied, no matter how much it looks for or learns.

Awareness does not need to be developed. It needs to realize itself. Everything follows from this.

True self knowledge is the Self of awareness knowing itself.

True salvation means awareness saving itself from unawareness.

When awareness is aware of being aware, it bypasses, surpasses, and encompasses the five senses. It sees them and is not them.

Attention is always drawn or controlled or forced, whereas awareness simply *is*.

Awareness is not something you *do*.

We *are* the awareness behind our body, mind, person, and all their experiences.

Pure awareness is who and what we are whether we are aware of it or not.

The Self of awareness encompasses and exists apart from everything it is aware of. It is simultaneously aware of everything and of itself being aware. This is what the absolute awareness in and of the universe is, and is always doing.

The mind of man is small and limited. It can envision the idea of pure awareness but cannot experience it.

The mind cannot be awareness.

Man thinks the universe and his life in it are about doing and achieving. But that is not what is behind the universe, and what encompasses the universe. That is not what makes the universe and everything in it possible.

The mystery of life is resolved as awareness comes to terms with itself.

The mind conceives of god in human form. It cannot do otherwise. Likewise, the mind conceives of awareness in mental form because it cannot do otherwise.

Pure, absolute awareness remains elusive except to itself as awareness.

God is not a divine person or personal agent. God does not say anything, do anything, give anything, or take anything away.

God is simply a term for the ocean of conscious awareness.

When we partake of awareness consciously, we partake of divinity which is just a religious term for the reality of utterly pure awareness.

Just as we are physically part of a larger physical universe, awareness is part of a larger awareness.

Simple, silent, conscious awareness emerges in, and merges with, itself.

God is a man-made idea and religion is a man-made belief system to support the idea.

There is really no need to believe anything, but for that you have to rely on awareness. Awareness has to rely on itself.

The notion of god is the mind's attempt to project a concept of the universe on its terms. Religion is then a result of the mind's attempt to make god tangible, moral, and responsible within that universe. It is all a strange construction once you see it for what it is.

The solution is to turn it all around and be wholly responsible for awareness. To render awareness more perceptible to itself.

Religion focuses on morality, virtue, and concepts of god, none of which have anything to do with the conscious awareness in and of the universe.

Religion keeps god outside and away from man, away from his true Self.

Ironically, religion binds awareness instead of freeing it.

Concepts and practices of religions tend to lead their followers away from the reality of what god is; away from what it means to reach god, to become one with god—to *become* awareness and consciously *be that*.

You cannot discover god without discovering the Self. Only then do you see the relationship. Only then do you see that the Self is not the feeling of 'I' or 'me', and that god is not out 'there'.

God is not about petitions, prayers, or actions. God is about awareness. God *is* awareness. It is just a term for the breadth, depth, and height of the purest awareness.

Men pray to god due to a limited understanding of what god is. True prayer, if it were needed, would let god alone the same way that god lets everything alone, and that would answer prayers in the best way.

Just let everything alone. Let it be the way it is and just see it. Letting go is a big relief.

God does not seek man. Awareness seeks itself. It essentially wants to be conscious of itself.

Curiously, the man or woman is not involved. It is an illusion, a mask.

God is fathomless awareness infinitely aware of being aware. This is incomprehensible to the mind, but not to awareness.

Absolute awareness does not act through anything. It is simply conscious of being aware of absolutely everything.

Despite all the scientific theories, we know next to nothing about the origins and manifestations and purposes of the universe. That we can be aware of being aware of this, however, starts to dissolve the enigma.

Thinking can take you to the edge, but the next step is out of thought into pure awareness. Into your Self.

Pure awareness is so subtle that you can hardly think about it without getting trapped in thought again. The best approach is to leave the mind alone and just let awareness be aware.

Awareness is its own purpose.

Everything, including awareness, is for awareness.

The human being is an incubator for awareness whose conscious realization and actualization is the climax of life on earth.

Becoming one with the universe means becoming aware of being aware.

The more that awareness becomes aware, the more it encompasses and the more oneness it comprises.

Conscious awareness leads to more devotion of awareness in others. This does not mean expressing or demonstrating 'love'. It means gratitude for being aware of awareness. Just appreciating that awareness exists.

Appreciation for being aware naturally spills over as love in feeling and in actions, but these are byproducts of awareness, not awareness itself.

Everything exists in relation *to* awareness and yet everything is a distraction *from* awareness. This is the miracle and its dilemma. We need both.

What we become aware *of* easily lures awareness away from the realization that we are aware and *are* awareness.

Awareness is not a point that becomes more solid as it becomes more aware. It is an imperceptible field that expands.

Man investigates what is in the universe and overlooks all the emptiness comprising it. He does the same with his psychological world.

It is hard to investigate emptiness.

Beyond everything is something that encompasses it. Infinite emptiness aware of all the fullness.

Awareness does not wait for anything because there is no time element in being aware of being aware. There is just being.

We see, hear, taste, touch, smell, think, feel, move, and react. Awareness is aware of all these and is none of them. It is also the only one that can be aware of itself.

Awareness can be aware that we are moving and speaking, thinking and hearing. Sometimes we realize this.

What we rarely realize is that this awareness can be aware of being aware—which implies something huge.

Thoughts are constantly pumped by the mind, and this pump cannot be stopped completely or for long. But that is not the point. The point is, where is awareness and what is it about?

Awareness does not think or speak. Nor is it an inner voice. It simply becomes aware that it is aware. Thoughts and words about it, such as "I am aware," are a deception.

Nothing that you can see inside or outside yourself is it.

Suffering can lead to awareness if you learn to accept suffering instead of complain and plead to god about it. The truth is that you are only complaining and pleading to awareness.

If, instead, you plead with awareness to be aware—to *be*—it will transcend the suffering. And the way to do that is simply to let it be *fully aware* of the suffering. The mind has to knowingly let go and yield completely to awareness.

Awareness exists outside the realms of happiness and sadness, pain and pleasure, gain and loss. Take all of these away and there it is.

At its best, suffering is a catalyst that enables awareness to get hold of itself.

The sense of 'me' intensifies with suffering and this intensity can heighten awareness which may in turn realize itself as the impartial witness to 'me' suffering. In this and other ways, awareness realizes that it is outside, and untouched by, everything.

When powerful emotions like anger and grief overwhelm us, it is not easy for awareness to remain aware of being aware. But if it does, it can surge to a higher realm of awareness. This is the intrinsic value of suffering and of using suffering as a catalyst to transcend emotions.

The number one problem with suffering is taking it personally. The number one problem with awareness is not taking it personally.

Do not glorify suffering. Glorify awareness.

The truth and true effect of awareness are not understood.

When you take awareness out of something, it loses meaning. When you put awareness into something, it fills up with meaning, which is particularly true when awareness puts itself into *itself*.

When you devote conscious awareness to a person or object or action, you give it life. The more awareness you devote, the more life you give it. If there is such a thing as a small miracle, this is it.

Awareness is everything. We are nothing without it.

Ordinarily, awareness unconsciously pours itself out of itself into thoughts, feelings, people, and things. Ordinary awareness is unconscious awareness.

When awareness is consciously aware, it extends itself without losing itself, and in this way fuels itself.

You are reborn when awareness reenters self-awareness. There is no other kind of rebirth.

When you are in a hurry for results, awareness loses hold of itself. It gets overrun by expectation, anxiety, irritation, worry, anger, fear—and a slew of other psychological habits.

The universe is never harried or hurried because it is not doing anything or going anywhere.

You can think about awareness, but only awareness can be aware.

Awareness is not a thought, feeling, sensation, or vision of any kind.

There is no end of things to be aware of, yet they all amount to nothing if awareness is not aware of being aware of them.

The most unique thing about the earth is that it is a laboratory for awareness. Even if such laboratories exist elsewhere, it still makes this one very rare, very precious.

It is a mystery that our bodies and minds physically appear out of nowhere, into conception, birth, and death.

It is even more of a mystery how awareness appears out of nothing, as nothing, into nothing. It is *no thing*.

This 'no thing' we call awareness is astonishing.

The infinite variety of the universe never compares to awareness being consciously aware.

Everything in our physical and psychological worlds serves as leverage for awareness to realize itself metaphysically.

If you force awareness, you lose it. You push it out of itself into the realm of thoughts, feelings, people, and activities. These things then start to matter more than awareness.

Our greatest loss is when awareness loses itself and *becomes* the thing it is aware of. This tendency to collapse out of itself evinces the delicate nature of awareness. Reversing this tendency is the single goal of spiritual evolution.

If you try to feel awareness or have others feel it, it becomes sensory. It falls to earth.

Awareness cannot be seen or shown. You cannot demonstrate that it is more real than any visible thing. The truth of it can only *be* experienced.

Perception is not awareness. Awareness is aware before, during, and after we perceive. But awareness is not naturally aware of being aware. This is the thing to grasp.

We get caught up in our physical, mental, and emotional reactions. Awareness does not. It is just aware.

Awareness is always one and the same when it gets hold of itself.

Awareness is not personal or possessive. Thus it causes no problems for itself.

The physical body appears, grows, deteriorates, and disappears, whereas awareness is ageless and timeless. Awareness silently realizes this about itself.

The inner feeling of 'me' is not awareness. That feeling is a psychological phantom. Awareness is aware of this and stands apart from it, neutrally encompassing it.

The feeling of who we are changes at home, at work, with friends or strangers, and at different ages of life. Awareness remains the same.

The purpose of life is to become aware of being aware. Nothing that we ever do will ever matter without this.

The physical eyes see, yet are unaware of seeing.

Awareness sees seeing, and is aware of doing so. Try to see this.

Awareness exists somewhere that science cannot understand.

Science is of the mind. Awareness is beyond.

Even the concept of 'now' is misleading because it implies time, whereas awareness is timeless.

Conscious awareness is conscious *of* the present. When this awareness becomes aware of itself, it brings astonishing clarity *to* the present.

Science, medicine, philosophy, psychology, and religion do not understand awareness. They study what awareness is aware *of* rather than studying its propensity to be aware of *itself*, and the implications of this.

Being aware of a sunset is fairly common. Being aware of watching a sunset is less common. Being aware of being aware of watching a sunset is the least common. And being aware of being aware of watching TV barely exists.

Awareness gets stuck in thoughts and feelings about whatever it becomes aware of. It has to learn to remain aware of itself as thoughts and feelings rise, crest, and fall away.

Everything rises, crests, and falls away *within* awareness.

When things 'come into' our awareness, they divert instantaneously into mental associations, daydreams, aspirations, fears, comparisons, and conclusions. Awareness gets imprisoned in this conglomeration of thoughts. How to avoid this imprisonment? This must be your personal discovery.

It is the exception for awareness *not* to be immersed in thought. When awareness steps out of this immersion, it witnesses the mystery of creation directly, without the filter of the mind.

Awareness sees the body hurt, sick, and aging and falsely believes that it is hurt, sick, and aging. In reality, it is just seeing the body.

Striving after, hoping for, and worrying about the future are all a result of being discontent with the present. But the discontentment is not with what is *in* the present; it is with a lack of awareness of being aware. When we focus on this, the present starts to fill up and the past and future begin to fade as the illusions they are.

Attention is an extension or outgrowth of awareness. It radiates outward from awareness, whereas awareness radiates in and as itself.

Attention is a stream of awareness while awareness is the whole ocean.

Alertness is not awareness. Alertness is acute attention.

Awareness is beyond attention and alertness, encompassing both.

When you are attentive, you project awareness in the form of noticing or doing something. When you are consciously aware, you impartially envelope the thing; you let the person or thing or action be itself *within* your awareness. There is no impulse to possess or change or control.

Awareness is just aware.

Attention becomes fixed on things and tries to manipulate them. Awareness always yields. Rather, it never clings.

As awareness becomes more conscious, the feeling of 'I' subsides. What seemed important becomes unimportant.

Judgment is harmful not because of any injury it does to who or what we judge, or to us for judging. The harm is in what it does to awareness.

Judgment, perhaps more than anything, sucks the life out of awareness and freezes perception.

Judgment belongs to the realm of thought and emotion. It lures awareness into this realm and corrupts it.

Conscious awareness is in stark contrast to judgment, which is a psychological posture of rejection. Learn to anticipate this and you will start to see differently.

The goal is not to eradicate judgment. The goal is for awareness to sustain its position of simply seeing what is in front of it without succumbing to the lure of judgment.

Nor does awareness judge judgment. It is aware of that lure, too.

People travel in the hope of living life more fully. But their hope is not realized because even though they are aware of more as they travel, awareness is not aware of being aware. Their travel is not fulfilling because awareness does not fulfill itself.

Emotions are perceptions that surge into reactions. Emotions are overrated pretenders.

Like thoughts, emotions are prompted by awareness but are not awareness itself.

The conviction of 'me' behind strong emotions is vacuous, yet it seems justifiably valid, which is why it is so hard to give up. The laughter. The tears. The awareness.

We are affected by our emotions. Awareness is not. It is simply aware of them.

Emotions have less pull when awareness is conscious of being aware of them. They lose their zest when they can no longer steal awareness.

Man does not awaken. Awareness awakens.

Awareness comes to and realizes that the identity of 'I' it was clinging to for so long is imaginary—nothing more than a mental image.

The Self, real I, the observer, the witness, third eye, higher centers, Big Mind, Buddha nature, Allah, Atman, Krishna, the Supreme, the other that I am. Awareness aware of being aware.

Meditation relaxes the mind and body, which can restore awareness. But meditation does not directly render awareness aware of itself. A mantra or method cannot do that.

Only awareness can render itself aware and be conscious of itself.

True meditation is not about holding a thought on something. It is about awareness residing as itself in itself.

In true meditation we do not meditate. Awareness does. And it can do it anywhere, anytime simply by being aware of itself.

True meditation supersedes thought the same way that awareness supersedes everything it is aware of.

Inner quietude is not awareness. Awareness resides beyond the quietude, encompassing it.

The solution to all problems is to be aware of being aware. In actuality, this does not solve all problems. It solves the most important problem.

Everything happens in relation to awareness, yet nothing happens in awareness itself.

As everything else appears, changes, and disappears, awareness remains the same.

When awareness is conscious of itself, being human means everything and nothing at the same time.

You are never what you are aware of, except when you become conscious of being aware.

Body, mind, sensations, and emotions mask the truth.

Attaching a name to the body attaches the notion of a person to it, and here the problem begins. Thoughts and emotions exacerbate the notion and the problem.

Awareness has no body, no name, no reputation, no accomplishments, no history, no nothing—yet it is everything.

It is frightening for our sense of 'I' to relinquish its identity because that identity is a false substitute. What sees this is real.

That we trust thought more than simple awareness tells the story of mankind.

You *can* trust awareness. Trust it. Trust it. Trust it.

Awareness does not try to identify or define itself. It has no concern whatsoever about that. It is not even busy trying to find itself because it already is itself.

Little children are very aware, but their awareness is not conscious of being aware. As they age, awareness moves farther from itself and closer to what it is aware of. In most cases, the closest thing it is aware of is the sense of 'I', 'me', 'mine' which gets projected internally and externally, and which petrifies as the person grows older.

When awareness becomes aware, it recognizes that it is becoming conscious. This is not a mental effort. It is a silent realization of awareness settling into itself and knowing itself again, which is one reason it feels so familiar and wonderful.

True detachment happens when awareness becomes conscious of the fact that it is not what it is aware of.

The only goal is for awareness just to *be*, without identifying itself with what it is aware of.

Attention unfolds. Perceptions come and go. Conscious awareness stays as it is and where it is, aware of everything unfolding, coming, and going.

Stress is a symptom of awareness having collapsed into the thing it is aware of. This results in psychological turmoil, which produces physical tension, which leads to illness. The deeper cause is not seen because we literally are not aware of it.

The strangest thing of all is that awareness in the human being is initially unaware of itself. It sets off on a course of being taken for granted—and overlooked—as the essential underpinning of *everything* else.

Everyone is searching for *who* they are without awareness knowing that it is *what* they really are.

Unaware, awareness gets stuck in different forms of identity, and the crisis begins.

Stop for a moment. Find the most quiet place in yourself. Silently comprehend that you accompany a body, with a mind, on a planet, in a vast space called the universe; that this existence includes the ability to be aware of it all, and that this awareness is the most remarkable thing about it all. Realize that all of it exists *inside* awareness, as *part of* awareness.

Awareness is not something you insist upon or force. It does not go after itself. It gives itself back to itself. It returns to itself. But these analogies don't suffice because, in actuality, awareness does not go out or return. It resides within itself.

Awareness does not try to mold things into a mental shape or force your life into an outcome. Awareness simply *is*.

Our body, thoughts, and emotions produce an irresistible urge to draw conclusions, resolve and accomplish, achieve and possess. In the midst of this, it is not easy to trust simple awareness as being more vital than thought and feeling, than body and possessions, than life itself. Yet it is far more vital.

There are many concepts about life and death, destiny and karma, angels and astral realms, visions and previous lives, enlightenment, and so on. But they mean little as long as we do not come to them through our own experience. And the only way to do that is with conscious awareness.

Awareness exists outside of past, present, and future. It is an all-encompassing vision that comprises the phenomena of time and space.

Usually unknown to itself, silent awareness peers through the prism of body, sensation, thought, and emotion, assuming that it is the prism. This is the untruth, the lie. As Omar Khayyam wrote: "One thing is certain and the rest is lies."

Just as awareness unconsciously collapses into and loses itself in whatever it becomes aware of, so it can consciously gather itself, know itself, and *encompass* everything it sees.

The internal and external worlds are not as our mind perceives them. They are multifaceted pieces of a single, unfathomable, unspeakable whole.

The truth is that everything stems from awareness and is a manifestation of awareness 'looking' at itself as a cue—a reminder—to be aware of being aware.

All true art emerges from the deep, silent, seemingly empty oasis of awareness. We do not 'create' art. It blooms of its own accord through our human being so that awareness (in ourselves and in others) may realize itself both in creation and as the source of creation.

This is why conscious awareness is able to comingle with everything. It is merely mingling with itself as itself, on very hallowed ground.

This is also why being aware of being aware is the greatest thing, and the only lasting thing, that anyone can ever do.

The higher you go, the more about awareness it all is.

Awareness *is* the mystery. There is only one.

Other books by Peter Ingle

OUR FATHER
The Inner Meaning of The Lord's Prayer

The Heart of Awareness

Transforming Negative Emotions

Think Before You Write

www.ingramcontent.com/pod-product-compliance
Lightning Source LLC
Chambersburg PA
CBHW020703300426
44112CB00007B/496